MW01489275

100
Foods by One

100 FIRST FOODS FOR BABY TO TRY BEFORE AGE 1

THANK YOU FOR YOUR PURCHASE!

★ ★ ★ ★ ★

WE WOULD REALLY APPRECIATE YOUR
REVIEW ON AMAZON!

Congratulations!

Congratulations on purchasing the '100 Foods By One' food diary! It's such an exciting time for you and your bub to begin this food journey together.

Why try 100 foods before age one?

- Greater variety of foods at an earlier age is suggested to reduce fussy eating at later stages
- There is growing evidence to suggest earlier exposure of allergens may reduce or prevent food allergies
- It's a great challenge to expose your little one to a wide range of taste and textures
- Trying different foods can be so much fun!

Things to remember:

Starting solids is recommended around 6 months of age, or more importantly when baby is showing signs of being ready. Speak with your maternal health nurse or paediatrician to discuss any questions or concerns.

How do I know when baby is ready?

- Great head and neck control, can sit upright
- Baby looks interested in food by staring at what you eat
- Reaching for your spoon or the food that's in your hand
- Baby is opening their mouth when you offer a spoon

This book offers a range of serving options for to consider. If a serving suggestion jumps out at you - just pop it into Google to find a recipe you'd like to try!

Recommended resources

Startingsolids.com - Fantastic website and phone app
Royal Childrens Hospital Melbourne: https://www.rch.org.au/
ASCIA - https://www.allergy.org.au/ - Allergy resources
Tiny Hearts Education - Facebook & Instagram - Baby & Child First Aid

Please note: This book is not offering professional health advice for your baby. Health advice changes frequently and differs by region in the world. This is a guide with ideas and is up to each parent or carer to research correct serving techniques and suitable foods for their child's individual eating abilities and age. ALWAYS watch your child and be within arms reach when eating. Be aware of potential allergens and have a plan in place should allergies present.

100 Foods Summary List

Fruits
- ☐ Apple
- ☐ Apricot
- ☐ Avocado
- ☐ Banana
- ☐ Blackberry
- ☐ Blueberry
- ☐ Cantaloupe
- ☐ Cherry
- ☐ Coconut
- ☐ Cranberry
- ☐ Fig
- ☐ Grapefruit
- ☐ Grapes
- ☐ Kiwifruit
- ☐ Lemon
- ☐ Lime
- ☐ Lychee
- ☐ Mandarin
- ☐ Mango
- ☐ Melon
- ☐ Nectarine
- ☐ Olive
- ☐ Orange
- ☐ Passionfruit
- ☐ Paw Paw
- ☐ Peach
- ☐ Pear
- ☐ Pineapple
- ☐ Plum
- ☐ Pomegranate
- ☐ Quince
- ☐ Raspberry
- ☐ Rhubarb
- ☐ Strawberry
- ☐ Tomato
- ☐ Watermelon

Vegetables
- ☐ Asparagus
- ☐ Beetroot
- ☐ Broccoli
- ☐ Brussels Sprouts
- ☐ Cabbage
- ☐ Carrots
- ☐ Cauliflower
- ☐ Celery
- ☐ Corn
- ☐ Cucumber
- ☐ Eggplant
- ☐ Garlic
- ☐ Green Beans
- ☐ Green Onion
- ☐ Kale
- ☐ Leek
- ☐ Lettuce
- ☐ Mushroom
- ☐ Onion (brown)
- ☐ Parsnip
- ☐ Peas
- ☐ Peppers
- ☐ Pickles
- ☐ Potato
- ☐ Pumpkin
- ☐ Sauerkraut
- ☐ Spinach
- ☐ Sweet Potato
- ☐ Seaweed
- ☐ Zucchini

Legumes
- ☐ Black Beans
- ☐ Chickpeas
- ☐ Kidney Beans
- ☐ Lentils

Protein
- ☐ Beef
- ☐ Chicken
- ☐ Eggs
- ☐ Goat
- ☐ Lamb
- ☐ Pork
- ☐ Salmon
- ☐ Sardines
- ☐ Shrimp/Prawn
- ☐ Tofu
- ☐ Turkey
- ☐ Venison

Grain
- ☐ Barley
- ☐ Bread (wheat)
- ☐ Cous Cous
- ☐ Oats
- ☐ Quinoa
- ☐ Rice

Dairy
- ☐ Cheddar Cheese
- ☐ Cottage Cheese
- ☐ Goats Cheese
- ☐ Greek Yoghurt
- ☐ Mozzarella
- ☐ Ricotta
- ☐ Sour Cream

Nuts
- ☐ Almond
- ☐ Cashew
- ☐ Hazelnut
- ☐ Macadamia
- ☐ Peanut

1. apple fruit

Tried (date)	Served as...	Liked	Disliked
11/01	Apple Puree	🙂	🙁
		🙂	🙁
		🙂	🙁
		🙂	🙁
		🙂	🙁

Serving Suggestions

- Apple and Pear Puree
- Apple Peanut Butter Porridge
- Oat & Apple Muffins
- Poached Apple & Cinnamon
- Apple & Berry Crumble

Notes: _____

2. apricot fruit

Tried (date)	Served as...	Liked	Disliked
		🙂	🙁
		🙂	🙁
		🙂	🙁
		🙂	🙁
		🙂	🙁

Serving Suggestions

- Apricot & Apple Puree
- Apricot Chicken
- Stewed Apricots & Yoghurt
- Thinly Sliced Fresh Apricot
- Apricot Jam On Toast

Notes: _____

3. avocado fruit

Tried (date)	Served as...	Liked	Disliked
		☺	☹
		☺	☹
		☺	☹
		☺	☹
		☺	☹

Serving Suggestions
- Avocado On Toast
- Avocado Spears
- Green Smoothie Bowl With Avocado
- Guacamole Dip
- Avocado & Coconut Icy Poles

Notes:

---

4. banana fruit

Tried (date)	Served as...	Liked	Disliked
		☺	☹
		☺	☹
		☺	☹
		☺	☹
		☺	☹

Serving Suggestions
- Creamy Banana Porridge
- Banana Muffins
- Banana Icecream
- Banana Buckwheat Pancakes
- Chopped Banana Pieces

Notes:

5. blackberry fruit

Tried (date)	Served as...	Liked	Disliked
		☺	☹
		☺	☹
		☺	☹
		☺	☹
		☺	☹

Serving Suggestions
- Sliced Blackberries
- Blackberry Yoghurt
- Blackberry & Apple Crumble Muffins
- Blackberry Scones
- Blackberry Jam On Toast

Notes: _____

6. blueberry fruit

Tried (date)	Served as...	Liked	Disliked
		☺	☹
		☺	☹
		☺	☹
		☺	☹
		☺	☹

Serving Suggestions
- Blueberries (cut or squashed)
- Blueberry Banana Smoothie
- Blueberry Muffins
- Blueberry Fruit Dip
- Blueberry Nicecream

Notes: _____

7. cantaloupe fruit

also known as rockmelon

Tried (date)	Served as...	Liked	Disliked
		☺	☹
		☺	☹
		☺	☹
		☺	☹
		☺	☹

Serving Suggestions

- Pureed Cantaloupe
- Banana & Cantaloupe Smash
- Cantoloupe Yoghurt
- Spiced Cantaloupe Loaf
- Cantaloupe Sorbet

Notes:

8. cherry fruit

Tried (date)	Served as...	Liked	Disliked
		☺	☹
		☺	☹
		☺	☹
		☺	☹
		☺	☹

Serving Suggestions

- Cherry Chia Seed Pudding
- Finely Chopped Cherries
- Stewed Cherry & Apple
- Cherry Yoghurt

Notes:

9. coconut fruit

Tried (date)	Served as...	Liked	Disliked
		☺	☹
		☺	☹
		☺	☹
		☺	☹
		☺	☹

Serving Suggestions

- Banana-Coconut Porridge
- Veggie Puree With Coconut Milk
- Mild Chicken Curry
- Coconut Water
- Coconut Rice

Notes:

10. cranberry fruit

Tried (date)	Served as...	Liked	Disliked
		☺	☹
		☺	☹
		☺	☹
		☺	☹
		☺	☹

Serving Suggestions

- Pear & Cranberry Puree
- Carrot & Cranberry Loaf
- Apple Cranberry Crumble
- Smushed Fresh Cranberries
- Shredded Turkey & Cranberry

Notes:

11. fig fruit

Tried (date)	Served as...	Liked	Disliked
		☺	☹
		☺	☹
		☺	☹
		☺	☹
		☺	☹

Serving Suggestions

- Avocado & Fig Puree
- Fig Jam on Toast
- Fresh Figs Smushed Or Cut
- Cinnamon & Fig Porridge
- Fig & Goats Cheese

Notes:

12. grapefruit fruit

Tried (date)	Served as...	Liked	Disliked
		☺	☹
		☺	☹
		☺	☹
		☺	☹
		☺	☹

Serving Suggestions

- Sliced Grapefruit
- Grapefruit and Banana Puree
- Grapefruit & Avocado Salad
- Grapefruit Yoghurt Cake

Notes:

13. grapes   fruit

Tried (date)	Served as...	Liked	Disliked
		☺	☹
		☺	☹
		☺	☹
		☺	☹
		☺	☹

Serving Suggestions

- Quartered Grapes
- Grape Jam on Toast
- Frozen Grapes (in mesh holder)

Notes: _____

14. kiwi fruit   fruit

Tried (date)	Served as...	Liked	Disliked
		☺	☹
		☺	☹
		☺	☹
		☺	☹
		☺	☹

Serving Suggestions

- Sliced Kiwifruit
- Green Kiwi & Apple Smoothie
- Strawberry Kiwi Nice Cream
- Kiwi Fruit Chia Pudding
- Kiwi & Banana Muffins

Notes: _____

15. lemon fruit

Tried (date)	Served as...	Liked	Disliked
		☺	☹
		☺	☹
		☺	☹
		☺	☹
		☺	☹

Serving Suggestions

- Try It Fresh! (Minimally)
- Lemon Juice On Fish
- Lemon & Raspberry Muffins
- Lemon Yoghurt Cake

Notes:

16. lime fruit

Tried (date)	Served as...	Liked	Disliked
		☺	☹
		☺	☹
		☺	☹
		☺	☹
		☺	☹

Serving Suggestions

- Try It Fresh! (Minimally)
- Lime Juice On Chicken Or Fish
- Lime Cake Bars
- Lime Dressing On Avocado
- Garlic & Lime Prawns

Notes:

17. lychee fruit

Tried (date)	Served as...	Liked	Disliked
		☺	☹
		☺	☹
		☺	☹
		☺	☹
		☺	☹

Serving Suggestions

(NOTE: Seed is poisonous, discard before serving)
- Sliced or Diced Lychee
- Lychee Sorbet

Notes: _____

18. mandarin fruit

Tried (date)	Served as...	Liked	Disliked
		☺	☹
		☺	☹
		☺	☹
		☺	☹
		☺	☹

Serving Suggestions

- Mandarin Pieces
- Porridge with Mandarin & Chia
- Mandarin Jam
- Mandarin & Almond Cake

Notes: _____

19. mango fruit

Tried (date)	Served as...	Liked	Disliked
		☺	☹
		☺	☹
		☺	☹
		☺	☹
		☺	☹

Serving Suggestions

- Mango Slices
- Mango Lassi
- Mango With Yoghurt
- Mango Chicken Curry
- Grilled Mango

Notes:

20. melon fruit

also known as honeydew melon

Tried (date)	Served as...	Liked	Disliked
		☺	☹
		☺	☹
		☺	☹
		☺	☹
		☺	☹

Serving Suggestions

- Honeydew Sorbet
- Melon Smoothie
- Ripe Melon Slices
- Frozen Melon In Mesh Feeder

Notes:

21. nectarine fruit

Tried (date)	Served as...	Liked	Disliked
		☺	☹
		☺	☹
		☺	☹
		☺	☹
		☺	☹

Serving Suggestions
- Ripe, Peeled Nectarine Pieces
- Grilled Nectarine & Cream
- Nectarine Cake
- Pear & Nectarine Puree

Notes:

22. olive fruit

Tried (date)	Served as...	Liked	Disliked
		☺	☹
		☺	☹
		☺	☹
		☺	☹
		☺	☹

Serving Suggestions
- Sliced Or Diced Pitted Olives
- Vegie Pizzas
- Olive & Avocado Dip
- Ground Olives On Bread
- Olive & Goats Cheese Dip

Notes:

23. orange fruit

Tried (date)	Served as...	Liked	Disliked
		☺	☹
		☺	☹
		☺	☹
		☺	☹
		☺	☹

Serving Suggestions

- Orange Pieces
- Orange & Oat Cookies
- Orange & Sweet Potato Puree
- Orange Cake
- Carrot & Orange Muffins

Notes:

24. passionfruit fruit

Tried (date)	Served as...	Liked	Disliked
		☺	☹
		☺	☹
		☺	☹
		☺	☹
		☺	☹

Serving Suggestions

- Passionfruit Yoghurt
- Passionfruit & Mango Smoothie
- Passionfruit On Pancakes
- Apple & Passionfruit Puree

Notes:

25. paw paw fruit

similar to papaya

Tried (date)	Served as...	Liked	Disliked
		☺	☹
		☺	☹
		☺	☹
		☺	☹
		☺	☹

Serving Suggestions

- Paw Paw Puree
- Mashed Paw Paw
- Frozen Paw Paw in Mesh Feeder
- Paw Paw Bread

Notes:

26. peach fruit

Tried (date)	Served as...	Liked	Disliked
		☺	☹
		☺	☹
		☺	☹
		☺	☹
		☺	☹

Serving Suggestions

- Peach Puree
- Peach Pancakes
- Grilled Peaches With Cream
- Avocado & Peach Dip
- Peach Porridge

Notes:

27. pear fruit

Tried (date)	Served as...	Liked	Disliked
		☺	☹
		☺	☹
		☺	☹
		☺	☹
		☺	☹

Serving Suggestions

- Stewed Pears & Cinnamon
- Pear & Apple Puree
- Thinly Sliced Ripe Pear
- Pear Porridge

Notes:

28. pineapple fruit

Tried (date)	Served as...	Liked	Disliked
		☺	☹
		☺	☹
		☺	☹
		☺	☹
		☺	☹

Serving Suggestions

- Fresh Pineapple
- Pineapple Mango Smoothie
- Pineapple & Peach Puree
- Frozen Pineapple In Mesh Feeder

Notes:

29. plum fruit

Tried (date)	Served as...	Liked	Disliked
		☺	☹
		☺	☹
		☺	☹
		☺	☹
		☺	☹

Serving Suggestions

- Ripe Sliced Plum
- Chopped Plum Porridge
- Stewed Plums
- Plum Pieces Rolled In Almond Flour
- Plum & Custard Cake

Notes:

30. pomegranate fruit

Tried (date)	Served as...	Liked	Disliked
		☺	☹
		☺	☹
		☺	☹
		☺	☹
		☺	☹

Serving Suggestions

- Squashed Pomegranate Arils
- Smashed Pomegranate and Avocado on Toast

Notes:

31. quince fruit

Tried (date)	Served as...	Liked	Disliked
		☺	☹
		☺	☹
		☺	☹
		☺	☹
		☺	☹

Serving Suggestions
- Quince Jam Sandwich
- Quince & Apple Puree
- Mango & Quince Sorbet
- Quince Paste On Rice Cakes
- Poached Quince & Mascarpone

Notes:

32. raspberry fruit

Tried (date)	Served as...	Liked	Disliked
		☺	☹
		☺	☹
		☺	☹
		☺	☹
		☺	☹

Serving Suggestions
- Cut Raspberries
- Raspberry Porridge
- Raspberry & Apple Puree
- Raspberry Banana Bread
- Raspberries & Yoghurt

Notes:

33. rhubarb fruit

Tried (date)	Served as...	Liked	Disliked
		☺	☹
		☺	☹
		☺	☹
		☺	☹
		☺	☹

Serving Suggestions (stalks only)

- Stewed Rhubarb & Peach
- Rhubarb & Cinnamon Porridge
- Rhubarb Crumble
- Rhubarb & Almond Muffins

Notes:

34. strawberry fruit

Tried (date)	Served as...	Liked	Disliked
		☺	☹
		☺	☹
		☺	☹
		☺	☹
		☺	☹

Serving Suggestions

- Strawberry & Apple Puree
- Strawberries In Mesh Feeder
- Thinly Sliced Fresh Strawberries
- Strawberries & Yoghurt

Notes:

35. tomato fruit

Tried (date)	Served as...	Liked	Disliked
		☺	☹
		☺	☹
		☺	☹
		☺	☹
		☺	☹

Serving Suggestions

- Boiled Tomato
- Tomato & Broccoli Puree
- Marinara Sauce & Pasta
- Chilli Con Carne (Mild)
- Tomato Mac 'n' Cheese

Notes:

36. watermelon fruit

Tried (date)	Served as...	Liked	Disliked
		☺	☹
		☺	☹
		☺	☹
		☺	☹
		☺	☹

Serving Suggestions

- Watermelon Smoothie
- Watermelon Sorbet
- Small Bite Sized Pieces
- Watermelon & Mozzarella Salad
- Frozen Watermelon In Feeder

Notes:

37. asparagus vegetable

Tried (date)	Served as...	Liked	Disliked
		☺	☹
		☺	☹
		☺	☹
		☺	☹
		☺	☹

Serving Suggestions

- Steamed Asparagus Spears
- Asparagus & Potato Puree
- Asparagus & Cheese Omelette
- Asparagus Soup

Notes:

38. beetroot vegetable

Tried (date)	Served as...	Liked	Disliked
		☺	☹
		☺	☹
		☺	☹
		☺	☹
		☺	☹

Serving Suggestions

- Thinly Sliced Cooked Beetroot
- Apple & Beetroot Puree
- Beetroot & Cheese Risotto
- Grated Beetroot In Salad

Notes:

39. broccoli vegetable

Tried (date)	Served as...	Liked	Disliked
		☺	☹
		☺	☹
		☺	☹
		☺	☹
		☺	☹

Serving Suggestions

- Steamed Broccoli Florets
- Cheesy Broccoli Balls
- Broccoli & Pumpkin Risotto
- Broccoli & Sweet Potato Puree

Notes:

40. brussels sprouts vegetable

Tried (date)	Served as...	Liked	Disliked
		☺	☹
		☺	☹
		☺	☹
		☺	☹
		☺	☹

Serving Suggestions

- Steamed Sprouts
- Sprouts, Carrot & Pumpkin Mash
- Pureed Sprouts
- Steamed Veggie Salad

Notes:

41. cabbage vegetable

Tried (date)	Served as...	Liked	Disliked
		☺	☹
		☺	☹
		☺	☹
		☺	☹
		☺	☹

Serving Suggestions

- Steamed Cabbage
- Chow Mein
- Cabbage Lasagne
- Veggie Pancakes
- Roast Cabbage Wedges

Notes:

42. carrot vegetable

Tried (date)	Served as...	Liked	Disliked
		☺	☹
		☺	☹
		☺	☹
		☺	☹
		☺	☹

Serving Suggestions

- Carrot Puree
- Steamed, Chopped Carrots
- Carrot & Sultana Muffins
- Homemade Carrot Cake

Notes:

43. cauliflower vegetable

Tried (date)	Served as...	Liked	Disliked
		☺	☹
		☺	☹
		☺	☹
		☺	☹
		☺	☹

Serving Suggestions
- Pureed Cauliflower
- Cauliflower & Broccoli Bake
- Cauliflower Rice
- Cauliflower Pizza Bases
- Cheesy Cauliflower Nuggets

Notes:

44. celery vegetable

Tried (date)	Served as...	Liked	Disliked
		☺	☹
		☺	☹
		☺	☹
		☺	☹
		☺	☹

Serving Suggestions
- Celery & Potato Puree
- Cooked and Sliced Celery
- Celery Soup
- Green Smoothie With Celery

Notes:

45. corn vegetable

Tried (date)	Served as...	Liked	Disliked
		☺	☹
		☺	☹
		☺	☹
		☺	☹
		☺	☹

Serving Suggestions
- Creamed Corn on Toast
- Corn On The Cob
- Pureed Corn, Carrot & Peas
- Chicken & Corn Soup
- Pumpkin & Corn Risotto

Notes: _____

46. cucumber vegetable

Tried (date)	Served as...	Liked	Disliked
		☺	☹
		☺	☹
		☺	☹
		☺	☹
		☺	☹

Serving Suggestions
- Thinly Sliced Cucumber
- Cucumber & Greek Yoghurt Dip

Notes: _____

47. eggplant vegetable

Tried (date)	Served as...	Liked	Disliked
		☺	☹
		☺	☹
		☺	☹
		☺	☹
		☺	☹

Serving Suggestions

- Eggplant Spears
- Baba Ganoush
- Eggplant & Sweet Potato Puree
- Grated Eggplant In Lasagne

Notes:

48. garlic vegetable

Tried (date)	Served as...	Liked	Disliked
		☺	☹
		☺	☹
		☺	☹
		☺	☹
		☺	☹

Serving Suggestions

- Minced Garlic Added To Recipes
- Garlic Bread

Notes:

49. green beans vegetable

Tried (date)	Served as...	Liked	Disliked
		☺	☹
		☺	☹
		☺	☹
		☺	☹
		☺	☹

Serving Suggestions

- Green Bean Puree
- Steamed Beans
- Smushed Bean, Carrot & Potato Fritters

Notes: _____

50. green onion vegetable

Tried (date)	Served as...	Liked	Disliked
		☺	☹
		☺	☹
		☺	☹
		☺	☹
		☺	☹

Serving Suggestions

- Finely Chopped In Omlette
- Diced On Top of Meals
- Spring Onion & Fetta Fritters
- Green Onion Cakes (bread)

Notes: _____

51. kale — vegetable

Tried (date)	Served as...	Liked	Disliked
		☺	☹
		☺	☹
		☺	☹
		☺	☹
		☺	☹

Serving Suggestions

- Steamed Kale
- Kale Omelette
- Apple & Kale Puree
- Kale Mac & Cheese

Notes:

52. leek — vegetable

Tried (date)	Served as...	Liked	Disliked
		☺	☹
		☺	☹
		☺	☹
		☺	☹
		☺	☹

Serving Suggestions

- Leek & Potato Soup
- Chicken & Leek Pie
- Leek & Sweet Potato Puree
- Salmon & Leek Parcels

Notes:

53. lettuce vegetable

Tried (date)	Served as...	Liked	Disliked
		☺	☹
		☺	☹
		☺	☹
		☺	☹
		☺	☹

Serving Suggestions

- Finely Shredded Lettuce
- Egg & Lettuce Sandwich
- Lettuce & Mince Cups
- Burrito Bowls

Notes:

54. mushroom vegetable

Tried (date)	Served as...	Liked	Disliked
		☺	☹
		☺	☹
		☺	☹
		☺	☹
		☺	☹

Serving Suggestions

- Mushroom Soup
- Roast Mushrooms & Veggies
- Mushroom & Pumpkin Risotto
- Mushroom & Chicken Puree

Notes:

55. onion (brown) vegetable

Tried (date)	Served as...	Liked	Disliked
		☺	☹
		☺	☹
		☺	☹
		☺	☹
		☺	☹

Serving Suggestions

- Chopped Onion In Fried Rice
- Caramelised Onion Risotto
- French Onion Soup
- Onion On Homemade Pizza

Notes: _____

56. parsnip vegetable

Tried (date)	Served as...	Liked	Disliked
		☺	☹
		☺	☹
		☺	☹
		☺	☹
		☺	☹

Serving Suggestions

- Parsnip & Apple Puree
- Roasted Parsnip Chips

Notes: _____

57. peas vegetable

Tried (date)	Served as...	Liked	Disliked
		☺	☹
		☺	☹
		☺	☹
		☺	☹
		☺	☹

Serving Suggestions

- Smashed Peas
- Pea & Corn Puree
- Pea Puree On Toast
- Squashed Pea & Tuna Casserole

Notes:

---

58. peppers vegetable

Also known as bell peppers or capsicum

Tried (date)	Served as...	Liked	Disliked
		☺	☹
		☺	☹
		☺	☹
		☺	☹
		☺	☹

Serving Suggestions

- Cooked Half
- Diced Peppers in Fried Rice
- Diced Peppers In Cous Cous

Notes:

59. pickles vegetable

Tried (date)	Served as...	Liked	Disliked
		☺	☹
		☺	☹
		☺	☹
		☺	☹
		☺	☹

Serving Suggestions

- Thin Sandwich Pickles on Bread
- Thin Pickle Spears
- Pickle Dip For Cauliflower Nuggets

Notes: _____

60. potato vegetable

Tried (date)	Served as...	Liked	Disliked
		☺	☹
		☺	☹
		☺	☹
		☺	☹
		☺	☹

Serving Suggestions

- Mashed Potato
- Potato Chips or Wedges
- Shepherds Pie
- Cheesy Scalloped Potato
- Tuna Jacket Potatos

Notes: _____

61. pumpkin vegetable

Tried (date)	Served as...	Liked	Disliked
		☺	☹
		☺	☹
		☺	☹
		☺	☹
		☺	☹

Serving Suggestions

- Pumpkin Puree
- Mashed Pumpkin
- Pumpkin Soup
- Pumpkin Bread
- Pumpkin & Cous Cous Fritters

Notes:

62. sauerkraut vegetable

Tried (date)	Served as...	Liked	Disliked
		☺	☹
		☺	☹
		☺	☹
		☺	☹
		☺	☹

Serving Suggestions

- Small Servings - Finely Chopped / Blended

Notes:

63. spinach vegetable

Tried (date)	Served as...	Liked	Disliked
		☺	☹
		☺	☹
		☺	☹
		☺	☹
		☺	☹

Serving Suggestions

- Finely Chopped Cooked Spinach
- Spinach & Cheese Omlette
- Spinach & Potato Mash
- Sweet Potato & Spinach Fritters

Notes:

64. sweet potato vegetable

Tried (date)	Served as...	Liked	Disliked
		☺	☹
		☺	☹
		☺	☹
		☺	☹
		☺	☹

Serving Suggestions

- Mashed Sweet Potato
- Sweet Potato Chips
- Sweet Potato Shepherds Pie
- Sweet Potato Veggie Burgers

Notes:

65. seaweed vegetable

Tried (date)	Served as...	Liked	Disliked
		☺	☹
		☺	☹
		☺	☹
		☺	☹
		☺	☹

Serving Suggestions

- Seaweed Flakes On Pasta
- Tuna & Seaweed Risotto
- Flakes On Mashed Potato
- Seaweed Flake Omelette

Notes:

66. zucchini vegetable

Tried (date)	Served as...	Liked	Disliked
		☺	☹
		☺	☹
		☺	☹
		☺	☹
		☺	☹

Serving Suggestions

- Zucchini Puree
- Zucchini Fritters
- Zucchini & Chicken Bites
- Zucchini Noodle Bolognaise

Notes:

67. beef protein

Tried (date)	Served as...	Liked	Disliked
		☺	☹
		☺	☹
		☺	☹
		☺	☹
		☺	☹

Serving Suggestions

- Pureed Beef
- Slow Cooked Beef Stew
- Beef & Vegetable Pies
- Meatballs
- Spaghetti Bolognaise

Notes: _____

68. chicken protein

Tried (date)	Served as...	Liked	Disliked
		☺	☹
		☺	☹
		☺	☹
		☺	☹
		☺	☹

Serving Suggestions

- Pureed Chicken & Veg
- Chicken Risotto
- Coconut Chicken Curry (mild)
- Chicken Drumsticks
- Chicken Fried Rice

Notes: _____

69. eggs  protein

Tried (date)	Served as...	Liked	Disliked
		☺	☹
		☺	☹
		☺	☹
		☺	☹
		☺	☹

Serving Suggestions
- Egg Sandwich
- Omelettes
- Scrambled Eggs On Toast
- Muffins / Cakes With Egg
- Vegetable Quiche

Notes:

70. goat protein

Tried (date)	Served as...	Liked	Disliked
		☺	☹
		☺	☹
		☺	☹
		☺	☹
		☺	☹

Serving Suggestions
- Goat Curry
- Pureed Goat's Meat
- Goat & Pumpkin Stew

Notes:

71. lamb protein

Tried (date)	Served as...	Liked	Disliked
		☺	☹
		☺	☹
		☺	☹
		☺	☹
		☺	☹

Serving Suggestions
- Mint & Lamb Puree
- Lamb & Veggie Rice
- Lamb & Pumpkin Mash
- Hearty Lamb Stew
- Slow Cooked Lamb Curry

Notes:

72. pork protein

Tried (date)	Served as...	Liked	Disliked
		☺	☹
		☺	☹
		☺	☹
		☺	☹
		☺	☹

Serving Suggestions
- Pork, Potato & Apple Puree
- Pork Bolognaise
- Pork Mince Patties
- Shredded Pork
- Lamb Casserole

Notes:

73. salmon protein

Tried (date)	Served as...	Liked	Disliked
		☺	☹
		☺	☹
		☺	☹
		☺	☹
		☺	☹

Serving Suggestions

- Mashed Salmon
- Salmon Patties
- Salmon & Spinach Risotto
- Smushed Salmon & Cous Cous
- Salmon & Avocado Sandwich

Notes: _____

74. sardines protein

Tried (date)	Served as...	Liked	Disliked
		☺	☹
		☺	☹
		☺	☹
		☺	☹
		☺	☹

Serving Suggestions

- Mashed Sardines On Toast
- Sardines & Cream Cheese
- Sardine Pasta Sauce
- Mushroom & Sardine Risotto

Notes: _____

75. shrimp / prawn — protein

Tried (date)	Served as...	Liked	Disliked
		☺	☹
		☺	☹
		☺	☹
		☺	☹
		☺	☹

Serving Suggestions

- Pureed Prawns & Avocado
- Prawn Aranchini Balls
- Prawn Toast
- Prawns In Fried Rice
- Prawn & Lemon Risotto

Notes: _____

76. tofu — protein

Tried (date)	Served as...	Liked	Disliked
		☺	☹
		☺	☹
		☺	☹
		☺	☹
		☺	☹

Serving Suggestions

- Tofu Nuggets
- Fruit & Tofu Smoothie
- Scrambled Tofu On Toast
- Silken Tofu Muffins

Notes: _____

77. turkey   protein

Tried (date)	Served as...	Liked	Disliked
		☺	☹
		☺	☹
		☺	☹
		☺	☹
		☺	☹

Serving Suggestions
- Pureed Turkey & Cranberries
- Shredded Turkey Roast
- Turkey & Avocado Patties
- Turkey & Vegetable Nuggets
- Turkey Mince Bolognaise

Notes:
_____

78. venison   protein
also: deer meat

Tried (date)	Served as...	Liked	Disliked
		☺	☹
		☺	☹
		☺	☹
		☺	☹
		☺	☹

Serving Suggestions
- Shredded Venison
- Venison Meatballs
- Venison Slow Cooked Stew
- Pureed Venison & Veg

Notes:
_____

79. barley   grain

Tried (date)	Served as...	Liked	Disliked
		☺	☹
		☺	☹
		☺	☹
		☺	☹
		☺	☹

Serving Suggestions

- Pearl Barley Risotto
- Barley Flour Pancakes
- Barley Flake Porridge
- Barley & Pumpkin Soup

Notes: _____

80. bread (wheat)   grain

Tried (date)	Served as...	Liked	Disliked
		☺	☹
		☺	☹
		☺	☹
		☺	☹
		☺	☹

Serving Suggestions

- Toast
- Sandwiches
- Bread & Butter Pudding
- French Toast
- Pizza Toast

Notes: _____

81. cous cous — grain

Tried (date)	Served as...	Liked	Disliked
		☺	☹
		☺	☹
		☺	☹
		☺	☹
		☺	☹

Serving Suggestions

- Cous Cous & Vegetables
- Warm Salmon & Dill Cous Cous
- Cous Cous Added To Salads
- Cous Cous & Egg Muffins

Notes:

82. oats — grain

Tried (date)	Served as...	Liked	Disliked
		☺	☹
		☺	☹
		☺	☹
		☺	☹
		☺	☹

Serving Suggestions

- Porridge
- Oat & Banana Muffins
- Healthy Oat Slice
- Blueberry Oat Bread
- Overnight Oats & Fruit

Notes:

83. quinoa grain

Tried (date)	Served as...	Liked	Disliked
		☺	☹
		☺	☹
		☺	☹
		☺	☹
		☺	☹

Serving Suggestions

- Quinoa & Pumpkin Puree
- Quinoa & Veggies
- Quinoa Beef Meatballs
- Overnight Quinoa

Notes:

84. rice grain

Tried (date)	Served as...	Liked	Disliked
		☺	☹
		☺	☹
		☺	☹
		☺	☹
		☺	☹

Serving Suggestions

- Fried Rice
- Muchroom Risotto
- Vegetarian Paella
- Rice Pudding
- Curried Rice

Notes:

85. cheddar cheese — dairy

Tried (date)	Served as...	Liked	Disliked
		☺	☹
		☺	☹
		☺	☹
		☺	☹
		☺	☹

Serving Suggestions

- Grated Cheese
- Cheese Toasty
- Mac & Cheese
- Cheesy Lasagne
- Cheesy Chicken Casserole

Notes:

---

86. cottage cheese — dairy

Tried (date)	Served as...	Liked	Disliked
		☺	☹
		☺	☹
		☺	☹
		☺	☹
		☺	☹

Serving Suggestions

- Plain Cottage Cheese
- Avocado & Cottage Cheese
- Cottage Cheese Pancakes
- Cottage Cheese Scrambled Eggs
- Cottage Cheese Pasta Sauce

Notes:

87. goats cheese — dairy

Tried (date)	Served as...	Liked	Disliked
		☺	☹
		☺	☹
		☺	☹
		☺	☹
		☺	☹

Serving Suggestions

- Crumbled Goats Cheese
- Goats Cheese Risotto
- Goats Cheese & Beetroot Salad
- Goats Cheese Tart
- Goats Cheese On Bread

Notes:

88. greek yoghurt — dairy

Tried (date)	Served as...	Liked	Disliked
		☺	☹
		☺	☹
		☺	☹
		☺	☹
		☺	☹

Serving Suggestions

- Greek Yoghurt & Fruit
- Greek Yoghurt & Berries, Frozen To Put In Mesh Feeder
- Greek Yoghurt Overnight Oats
- Greek Yoghurt Banana Smoothie

Notes:

89. mozzarella dairy

Tried (date)	Served as...	Liked	Disliked
		☺	☹
		☺	☹
		☺	☹
		☺	☹
		☺	☹

Serving Suggestions

- Fresh Mozzarella
- Crumbed Mozzarella Sticks
- Mozzarella & Pesto Pasta
- Pizza Toast

Notes: _____

90. ricotta dairy

Tried (date)	Served as...	Liked	Disliked
		☺	☹
		☺	☹
		☺	☹
		☺	☹
		☺	☹

Serving Suggestions

- Ricotta & Pureed Peach
- Lemon Ricotta Pasta
- Ricotta On Toast
- Ricotta In Cannelloni
- Ricotta Fruit Cake

Notes: _____

91. sour cream dairy

Tried (date)	Served as...	Liked	Disliked
		☺	☹
		☺	☹
		☺	☹
		☺	☹
		☺	☹

Serving Suggestions

- Served On Potato Wedges
- Sour Cream Dip
- Sour Cream & Chicken Sandwich
- Sour Cream Scrambled Eggs
- Sour Cream Blueberry Muffins

Notes:

92. almond nuts

Tried (date)	Served as...	Liked	Disliked
		☺	☹
		☺	☹
		☺	☹
		☺	☹
		☺	☹

Serving Suggestions

- Almond Butter & Greek Yoghurt
- Ground Almonds On Porridge
- Almond Butter On Toast
- Almond Meal Muffins

Notes:

93. cashew nuts

Tried (date)	Served as...	Liked	Disliked
		☺	☹
		☺	☹
		☺	☹
		☺	☹
		☺	☹

Serving Suggestions

- Cashew Butter On Toast
- Cashew Ground On Curry
- Cashew Butter Chicken Stew
- Fruit Dipped In Cashew Butter
- Cashew Butter Porridge

Notes: _____

94. hazelnut nuts

Tried (date)	Served as...	Liked	Disliked
		☺	☹
		☺	☹
		☺	☹
		☺	☹
		☺	☹

Serving Suggestions

- Hazelnut Butter On Toast
- Hazelnut Butter Overnight Oats
- Hazelnut Butter Smoothie
- Hazelnut Flour Cookies
- Hazelnut & Apple Muffins

Notes: _____

95. macadamia nuts

Tried (date)	Served as...	Liked	Disliked
		☺	☹
		☺	☹
		☺	☹
		☺	☹
		☺	☹

Serving Suggestions

- Macadamia Butter Dip
- Macadamia Curry Sauce
- Macadamia Banana Smoothie
- Macadamia & Cacao Spread

Notes:

96. peanut nuts

Tried (date)	Served as...	Liked	Disliked
		☺	☹
		☺	☹
		☺	☹
		☺	☹
		☺	☹

Serving Suggestions

- Peanut Butter Toast
- Peanut Butter Porridge
- Peanut Butter + Banana Smoothie
- Peanut Butter Oatmeal Cookies

Notes:

97. black beans legumes

Tried (date)	Served as...	Liked	Disliked
		☺	☹
		☺	☹
		☺	☹
		☺	☹
		☺	☹

Serving Suggestions
- Black Bean Dip
- Black Bean Loaded Potatos
- Bean & Quinoa w/ Veg
- Bean & Cheese Quesadilla

Notes:

98. chickpeas legumes

Tried (date)	Served as...	Liked	Disliked
		☺	☹
		☺	☹
		☺	☹
		☺	☹
		☺	☹

Serving Suggestions
- Pumpkin & Chickpea Mash
- Hummus & Pita Bread
- Chickpea & Sweet Potato Dahl
- Veggie Soup With Chickpeas

Notes:

99. kidney beans legumes

Tried (date)	Served as...	Liked	Disliked
		☺	☹
		☺	☹
		☺	☹
		☺	☹
		☺	☹

Serving Suggestions

- Bean Casserole
- Kidney Bean Fritters
- Homemade Baked Beans
- Bean Puree on Crackers

Notes:

100. lentils legumes

Tried (date)	Served as...	Liked	Disliked
		☺	☹
		☺	☹
		☺	☹
		☺	☹
		☺	☹

Serving Suggestions

- Lentil & Sweet Potato Puree
- Curried Lentil Bake
- Lentil Broccoli Bites
- Lentil Meatballs

Notes:

Tried (date)	Served as...	Liked	Disliked
		😊	😞
		😊	😞
		😊	😞
		😊	😞
		😊	😞

Notes:

Tried (date)	Served as...	Liked	Disliked
		😊	😞
		😊	😞
		😊	😞
		😊	😞
		😊	😞

Notes:

Tried (date)	Served as...	Liked	Disliked
		☺	☹
		☺	☹
		☺	☹
		☺	☹
		☺	☹

Notes:

Tried (date)	Served as...	Liked	Disliked
		☺	☹
		☺	☹
		☺	☹
		☺	☹
		☺	☹

Notes:

Tried (date)	Served as...	Liked	Disliked
		☺	☹
		☺	☹
		☺	☹
		☺	☹
		☺	☹

Notes:

Tried (date)	Served as...	Liked	Disliked
		☺	☹
		☺	☹
		☺	☹
		☺	☹
		☺	☹

Notes:

Tried (date)	Served as...	Liked	Disliked
		☺	☹
		☺	☹
		☺	☹
		☺	☹
		☺	☹

Notes:

Tried (date)	Served as...	Liked	Disliked
		☺	☹
		☺	☹
		☺	☹
		☺	☹
		☺	☹

Notes:

Tried (date)	Served as...	Liked	Disliked
		☺	☹
		☺	☹
		☺	☹
		☺	☹
		☺	☹

Notes: _____

Tried (date)	Served as...	Liked	Disliked
		☺	☹
		☺	☹
		☺	☹
		☺	☹
		☺	☹

Notes: _____

Tried (date)	Served as...	Liked	Disliked
		☺	☹
		☺	☹
		☺	☹
		☺	☹
		☺	☹

Notes: _____

Tried (date)	Served as...	Liked	Disliked
		☺	☹
		☺	☹
		☺	☹
		☺	☹
		☺	☹

Notes: _____

Tried (date)	Served as...	Liked	Disliked
		☺	☹
		☺	☹
		☺	☹
		☺	☹
		☺	☹

Notes:

Tried (date)	Served as...	Liked	Disliked
		☺	☹
		☺	☹
		☺	☹
		☺	☹
		☺	☹

Notes:

Tried (date)	Served as...	Liked	Disliked
		☺	☹
		☺	☹
		☺	☹
		☺	☹
		☺	☹

Notes:

Tried (date)	Served as...	Liked	Disliked
		☺	☹
		☺	☹
		☺	☹
		☺	☹
		☺	☹

Notes:

Tried (date)	Served as...	Liked	Disliked
		☺	☹
		☺	☹
		☺	☹
		☺	☹
		☺	☹

Notes:

Tried (date)	Served as...	Liked	Disliked
		☺	☹
		☺	☹
		☺	☹
		☺	☹
		☺	☹

Notes:

Tried (date)	Served as...	Liked	Disliked
		☺	☹
		☺	☹
		☺	☹
		☺	☹
		☺	☹

Notes:

Tried (date)	Served as...	Liked	Disliked
		☺	☹
		☺	☹
		☺	☹
		☺	☹
		☺	☹

Notes:

ADDITIONAL FOODS

Made in United States
Orlando, FL
03 April 2025

60126620R00036